Burns und Lambert

Catholic Hymns

Burns und Lambert

Catholic Hymns

ISBN/EAN: 9783741176210

Manufactured in Europe, USA, Canada, Australia, Japa

Cover: Foto ©Lupo / pixelio.de

Manufactured and distributed by brebook publishing software
(www.brebook.com)

Burns und Lambert

Catholic Hymns

Catholic Hymns,

ARRANGED IN ORDER FOR
THE CHIEF FESTIVALS, THE FEASTS OF SAINTS, ETC.,
THROUGHOUT THE YEAR.

WITH ILLUSTRATIONS.

NEW EDITION,
REVISED AND ENLARGED.

LONDON:
BURNS AND LAMBERT.

Advertisement

THE Hymns are given in the same order in the following
reprint as in the preceding smaller edition, in order to
prevent confusion with the corresponding volume of music
adapted to it. The feature of novelty in the present edition
is the addition of a select number of fresh Hymns that
have become popular and well known

The Hymns contained in this collection are, with but few
exceptions, the production of living Catholic authors, and
a large proportion of them are original. The few Hymns
to which no author's name is affixed have been selected
from different Catholic Hymn-books in use in the dioceses
of the United States of America. These have been care-
fully revised, and in some instances cast into almost an
entirely new form. One or two well-known hymns by Father
Faber have, with the author's permission, been varied
slightly, for the sake of the tune, from the original text.
The Hymns for " The Assumption," " May Jesus Christ be
praised!" "Divine Grace," " The Last Farewell," come
from the pen of the Rev. Father Caswall, and the " Hymn
for the Month of May" from the pen of Dr. Newman. The
Editors also feel a pleasure in being allowed to add, that
the poems of this collection, and also of the Catholic
Sacred Songs, signed " Sister M. J." in the table of contents,
are due to the talent and piety of a member of the Convent
of Sisters of Mercy, at Charleville, in the County of Cork.

TABLE OF CONTENTS.

In Alphabetical order, referring to the Title of each Hymn.

"See down His face and neck and breast
His sacred blood descend."—p. 14.

HYMNS

FOR

MORNING AND EVENING.

———

1.   𝕸𝖔𝖗𝖓𝖎𝖓𝖌 𝕳𝖞𝖒𝖓.

Now doth the sun ascend the sky,
　And wake creation with its ray:
Be present with us, Lord most high,
　Through all the actions of the day.

Create in us a heart sincere,
　Simplicity of word and will;
And may the morn, so pure, so clear,
　Its own sweet calm in us instil.

Keep us, eternal Lord, this day,
　From every sinful passion free;
Grant us in all we do and say,
　In all our thoughts, to honour Thee

For all day long on heaven's high tower
　There stands Thy sentinel, who spies
Our every action hour by hour,
　From early dawn till daylight dies

So when the evening stars appear,
  And in their train the darkness bring
May we, O Lord, with conscience clear
  To Thee our grateful praises sing

---

2.   Evening Hymn.

O LORD of perfect purity,
  Who dost the world with light adorn,
And paint the fields of azure sky
  With lovely hues of eve and morn ·

Upon our fainting souls distil
  The grace of Thy celestial dew;
Let no fresh snare to sin beguile,
  No former sin revive anew

Keep Thou our souls from schemes of crime,
  No guilt remorseful let them know;
Nor, thinking but on things of time,
  Into eternal darkness go

Teach us to knock at heav'n s high door;
  Teach us the prize of life to win;
Teach us all evil to abhor,
  And purify ourselves within.

Be Thou our guide, be Thou our goal,
  Be Thou our pathway to the skies
Our joy when sorrow fills the soul,
  In death our everlasting prize.

HYMNS

FOR THE

PRINCIPAL FESTIVALS OF THE YEAR.

---

3.   **Advent Hymn.**

CREATOR of the starry frame,
   Eternal light of all who live;
Jesu, Redeemer of mankind,
   An ear to Thy poor suppliants give.

When man, o'erwhelm'd in sin and death,
   Was wholly lost in Satan's snare,
Love brought Thee down to cure our ills,
   By taking of those ills a share.

Thy love for guilty men it was
   That caused Thy sacred blood to flow;
When issuing from Thy virgin shrine,
   Thou didst to death a victim go.

Great Judge of all, in that last day
   When friends shall fail and foes combine,
Look down in pity then, we pray,
   And guard us with Thine arm divine.

To God the Father and the Son
  All praise and power and glory be,
With Thee, O sacred Paraclete,
  Both now and through eternity

---

4.   Christmas Hymn.

(I.)

Sing, my tongue, the Saviour's glory,
  Sing with joy and holy mirth;
Tell aloud the famous story
  Of His spotless virgin birth;
How He comes, an infant stranger,
  Here to dwell with us on earth.

Now the long-expected fulness
  Of the sacred time draws nigh;
Now for us the Word eternal
  Leaves His Father's throne on high;
From a virgin's womb appearing,
  Cloth'd in our mortality.

All within a lowly manger,
  Lo. a helpless Babe He lies;
See, His gentle virgin Mother
  Lull to sleep His infant cries,
While the limbs of God incarnate
  Round with swathing bands she ties

Blessing, honour everlasting
  To th' immortal Deity;
To the Father, Son, and Spirit,
  Equal adoration be.
Praised be Thou through earth and heaven,
  Sempiternal Unity

5. Christmas Hymn.

(II.)

SEE amid the winter's snow,
Born for us on earth below,
See the tender Lamb appears,
Promis'd from eternal years.
    Hail, thou ever-blessed morn!
    Hail, redemption's happy dawn:
    Sing through all Jerusalem,
    Christ is born in Bethlehem!

Lo, within a manger lies
He who built the starry skies;
He who, thron'd in height sublime,
Sits amid the cherubim
    Hail, &c.

"Say, ye holy shepherds, say
What your joyful news to-day?
Wherefore have ye left your sheep
On the lonely mountain steep?"
    Hail, &c.

"As we watch'd at dead of night,
Lo! we saw a wondrous light;
Angels singing, 'Peace on earth,'
Told us of the Saviour's birth."
    Hail, &c.

Sacred Infant! all divine!
What a tender love was Thine,
Thus to come from highest bliss
Down to such a world as this!
    Hail, &c.

Teach, oh, teach us, holy Child,
By Thy face so meek and mild;
Teach us to resemble thee
In Thy sweet humility.
    Hail, &c.

Virgin Mother! Mary blest!
By the joys that fill thy breast,
Pray for us, that we may prove
Worthy of the Saviour's love
    Hail, &c.

6.　　　Holy Innocents.

LOVELY flowers of martyrs, hail!
  Smitten by the tyrant foe,
On life's threshold,—as the gale
  Strews the roses ere they blow.

First to die for Christ—sweet lambs,
  At the very altar ye,
With your fatal crowns and palms,
  Sport in your simplicity.

Yet is Herod's wrath in vain,
  Though a thousand babes he slay;
Christ, amid a thousand slain,
  Is in safety borne away.

Honour, virtue, glory, merit,
  Be to thee, O Virgin's Son,
With the Father and the Spirit,
  While eternal ages run.

7. Hymn for the Epiphany.

BETHLEHEM, of noblest cities
None can once with thee compare,
Thou alone the Lord from heaven
Didst for us incarnate bear.
Fairer than the beam of morning
Was the star that told His birth,
To the lands their God announcing,
Hid beneath a form of earth.

By its lambent beauty guided,
See the Eastern kings appear;
See them bend their gifts to offer,
Purest incense, gold, and myrrh,
Sacred gifts of mystic meaning;
Incense doth the God disclose,
Gold a royal child proclaimeth,
Myrrh a future tomb foreshews.

Holy Jesu, in Thy brightness
To the Gentile world reveal'd,
Still to babes Thyself disclosing,
Ever from the proud conceal'd;
Honour, glory, virtue, merit,
Be to Thee, O Virgin's Son,
With the Father and the Spirit,
While eternal ages run.

---

8. The Holy name of Jesus.

JESU, the very thought of Thee
With sweetness fills my breast;
But sweeter far Thy face to see,
And in Thy presence rest.

Nor voice can sing, nor heart can frame,
  Nor can the memory find
A sweeter sound than Thy blest Name,
  O Saviour of mankind.

O, Jesu, Thou the beauty art
  Of angel worlds above;
Thy Name is music to the heart,
  Enchanting it with love.

O hope of every contrite soul,
  O joy of all the meek,
How kind art Thou to those who fall,
  How good to those who seek!

But what to those who find? ah, this
  Nor tongue nor pen can shew:
The love of Jesus, what it is,
  None but His lov'd ones know.

O Jesu, spotless Virgin flower,
  Our life, our joy, to Thee
Be praise, beatitude, and power
  Through all eternity.

9.   Hymn for Good Friday.

O'erwhelm'd in depths of woe,
  With racking anguish torn,
Behold the Saviour of mankind
  Upon the tree of scorn.
See how the nails those hands
  And feet so tender rend;
See down His face and neck and breast
  His sacred blood descend.

Hark with what awful cry
He yields His parting breath!
That cry it steeps His mother's soul
As in a swoon of death.
The sun withdraws his beam,
The mid-day heav'ns grow pale,
The moon, the stars, the universe,
Their Maker's death bewail.

Shall man alone be mute,
Amidst adoring spheres?
Come, old and young, come, rich and poor,
And bathe those feet in tears
Come kneel before His Cross,
Who shed for us His blood;
Who died the victim of pure love,
To make us sons of God.

10.　　　　Easter Hymn.

(i.)

Victimæ Paschali laudes:

CHRIST the Lord is ris'n to-day:
Christians, haste your vows to pay;
Offer ye your praises meet
At the Paschal Victim's feet.
For the sheep the Lamb hath bled,
Sinless in the sinner's stead;
Christ the Lord is ris'n on high,
Now He lives no more to die.

Christ, the victim undefil'd,
Man to God hath reconcil'd;
Whilst in strange and awful strife
Met together Death and Life.

Christians, on this happy day
Haste with joy your vows to pay;
Christ the Lord is ris'n on high,
Now He lives no more to die.

Say, O wond'ring Mary, say,
What thou sawest on thy way?
" I beheld, where Christ had lain,
Empty tomb and angels twain;
   I beheld the glory bright
   Of the rising Lord of light:
   Christ my hope is ris'n again,
   Now He lives, and lives to reign."

Christ, who once for sinners bled,
Now the firstborn from the dead,
Thron'd in endless might and power,
Lives and reigns for evermore.
   Hail, eternal hope on high!
   Hail, Thou King of victory!
   Hail, Thou Prince of life ador'd!
   Help and save us, gracious Lord!

---

11.   Easter Hymn.

(II.)

O filii et filiæ.

Ye sons and daughters of the Lord!
The King of glory, King ador'd,
This day Himself from death restor'd

All in the early morning grey
Went holy women on their way,
To see the tomb where Jesus lay.

Of spices pure a precious store
In their pure hands those women bore,
To anoint the sacred Body o'er.

Then straightway one in white they see,
Who saith, "The Lord is ris'n, and He
Precedes you into Galilee."

This told they Peter, told they John,
Who forthwith to the tomb are gone,
But Peter is by John outrun.

That selfsame night, while out of fear
The doors were shut, their Lord most dear
To His Apostles did appear.

But Thomas, when of this he heard,
Was doubtful of his brethren's word;
Wherefore again there comes the Lord

"Thomas, behold my side," saith He;
"My hands, my feet, my body see,
And doubt not, but believe in me"

When Thomas saw that wounded side,
The truth no longer he denied;
"Thou art my Lord and God!" he cried.

Oh blest are they who have not seen
Their Lord, and yet believe in Him!
Eternal life awaiteth them.

Now let us praise the Lord most high,
And strive His name to magnify
On this great day through earth and sky.

Whose mercy ever runneth o'er;
Whom men and angel hosts adore;
To Him be glory evermore.

12. Feast of the Ascension.

O THOU eternal King most high,
　Who didst the world redeem;
And conquering death and hell, receive
　A dignity supreme:

This day beheld Thee through the skies
　To Thy bright throne ascend;
Thenceforth to reign in sovereign power,
　And glory without end.

There, seated in Thy majesty,
　To Thee submissive bow
The spacious earth, the highest heaven,
　The depths of hell below.

With trembling there the angels see
　The chang'd estate of man;
The flesh which sinn'd by Flesh redeem'd,
　And Man o'er seraphs reign.

There, waiting for Thy faithful souls,
　Be Thou to us, O Lord,
Our peerless joy while here we stay,
　In heav'n our great reward.

13. Hymn for Pentecost.

HOLY Spirit. Lord of light,
From Thy clear celestial height
　Thy pure beaming radiance give.
Come, Thou Father of the poor,
Come with treasures which endure,
　Come, Thou light of all that live

Thou, of all consolers best,
Thou, the soul's delightful guest,
　　Dost refreshing peace bestow;
Thou in toil art comfort sweet,
Pleasant coolness in the heat,
　　Solace in the midst of woe

Light immortal, Light divine,
Visit Thou these hearts of thine,
　　And our inmost being fill;
If Thou take Thy grace away,
Nothing pure in man will stay—
　　All his good is turn'd to ill.

Heal our wounds, our strength renew,
On our dryness pour Thy dew,
　　Wash the stains of guilt away,
Bend the stubborn heart and will,
Melt the frozen, warm the chill,
　　Guide the steps that go astray.

Thou on those who evermore
Thee confess and Thee adore,
　　In Thy sevenfold gifts descend;
Give them comfort when they die,
Give them life with Thee on high,
　　Give them joys which never end.

———————

14. *Feast of Corpus Christi.*

Sing, my tongue, the Saviour's glory,
　　Of His flesh the mystery sing;
Of the blood, all price exceeding,
　　Shed by our immortal king;
Destin'd, for the world's redemption
　　From a noble womb to spring.

Of a pure and spotless Virgin
   Born for us on earth below,
He, as man with man conversing,
   Stay'd the seeds of truth to sow;
Then He clos'd in solemn order
   Wondrously His life of woe.

On the night of that last supper,
   Seated with His chosen band,
He, the Paschal victim eating,
   First fulfils the law's command.
Then, as food to all His brethren,
   Gives Himself with His own hand.

Word made flesh, the bread of nature
   By His word to flesh He turns,
Wine into His blood He changes:
   What though sense no change discerns?
Only be the heart in earnest,
   Faith her lesson quickly learns.

Down in adoration falling,
   Lo, the sacred Host we hail;
Lo, o'er ancient forms departing,
   Newer rites of grace prevail;
Faith for all defects supplying,
   Where the feeble senses fail.

To the everlasting Father,
   And the Son who reigns on high,
With the Holy Ghost proceeding
   Forth from each eternally,
Be salvation, honour, blessing,
   Might, and endless majesty.

15. Feast of the Most Sacred Heart of Jesus.

Jesu, Creator of the world,
  Of all mankind Redeemer blest;
True God of God, in whom we see
  The Father's image clear express'd:

Thee, Saviour, love alone constrain'd
  To make our mortal flesh Thine own;
And as a second Adam come,
  For the first Adam to atone.

That selfsame love which made the sky,
  Which made the sea, the stars, and earth
Took pity on our misery,
  And broke the bondage of our birth.

O Jesu, in Thy heart divine
  May that same love for ever glow;
For ever mercy to mankind
  From that exhaustless fountain flow!

For this Thy sacred heart was pierced,
  And both with blood and water ran;
To cleanse us from the stains of guilt,
  And be the hope and strength of man.

To God the Father and the Son,
  All praise, and power, and glory be
With Thee, O holy Paraclete,
  Both now and through eternity.

HYMNS

APPROPRIATE TO

THE FEASTS OF PARTICULAR SAINTS.

---

16. Hail, holy Joseph, Hail.

(St. Joseph, spouse of the Blessed Virgin Mary,
March 19th.)

HAIL, holy Joseph, hail!
  Chaste spouse of Mary, hail!
Pure as the lily flower
  In Eden's peaceful vale

Hail, holy Joseph, hail!
  Prince of the house of God!
May His best graces be
  By thy sweet hands bestow'd.

Hail, holy Joseph, hail!
  Belov'd of angels, hail!
Cheer thou the hearts that faint,
  And guide the steps that fail

Hail, holy Joseph, hail!
  God's choice wert thou alone,
To thee the Word made flesh
  Was subject as a Son.

O Christ's dear Mother, bless;
  And bless, ye Saints on high,
All meek and simple souls
  That to Saint Joseph cry.

17. Feast of the Annunciation of B. V. M.

(March 25th.)

What mortal tongue can sing thy praise,
  Dear mother of the Lord?
To angels only it belongs,
  Thy glory to record.

Say, Mary, what sweet force was that
  Which from the Father's breast
Drew forth His co-eternal Son,
  To be thy bosom's guest?

'Twas not thy guileless faith alone
  That lifted thee so high;
'Twas not thy pure seraphic love,
  Or peerless chastity

But oh! it was thy lowliness,
  Well pleasing to the Lord,
That made thee worthy to become
  The mother of the Word.

O loftiest, whose humility
  So sweet it was to see,
That God, forgetful of Himself,
  Abased Himself to thee.

---

18. St. Aloysius.

(June 21st.)

Dear Saint, who on thy natal day
  To Mary's tender care was given,
And did beneath her gentle sway
  Almost unsinning pass to heav'n:

Sweet flower which lov'd to bloom unknown;
  A Saint 'mid worldly pomp and pride;
Who at the footstep of a throne
  Knew nought but Jesus crucified:

Blest youth, who cast a crown away,
  To bo with Christ despised and poor
Teach us to walk our humble way,
  Content, though little be our store

May no repining fill our breast
  Amid the ills of poverty;
Oh, make us feel that we are blest,
  To be thus poor with Christ and thee!

Teach us like thee to shrink from sin,
  Like thee to love sweet purity;
That we from Mary's heart may win
  The love she once bestowed on thee

Thus safe beneath her gentle sway,
  Oh, may the grace to us be giv'n,
To pass from earth some happy day,
  And join thee in the courts of heav'n

---

19. St. Anne, Mother of the
B. V. Mary.
(July 26th.)

SPOTLESS Anna, Juda's glory,
  Through the Church from east to west
Every tongue proclaims thy praises,
  Holy Mary's mother blest!

Saintly kings and priestly sires
  Blended in thy sacred line;

'Thou in virtue all before thee
Didst excel by grace divine.

Link'd in bonds of purest wedlock,
Thine it was for us to bear,
By the favour of high heaven,
Our immortal Virgin star.

From thy stem in beauty budded
Ancient Jesse's mystic rod;
Earth from thee received the mother
Of the eternal Son of God.

All the human race benighted
In the depths of darkness lay,
When in Anne it saw the dawning
Of the long-expected day.

20. Feast of the Assumption of the B. V. Mary.

(August 15th.)

See, to God's high temple above
Mounts amid angel hymns of love,
　　The mystical ark of grace:
See aloft on victory's throne,
Blended in glory both Mother and Son,
　　In one eternal embrace!

All the sorrows her bosom bore,
All her pains and afflictions sore,
　　At length supremely repaid;—
There she reigns on the cloudless height,
Only less than the Lord of light,
　　In hues immortal arrayed.

There she lives as a fount of grace,
Ever flowing for Adam's race,
    And still for ever to flow;
There, while ages on ages run,
Sweetly, sweetly, she pleads with her Son
    For us her children below.

Lady, than all the heavens more high,
More than seraph in purity,
    A glance of pity incline!
Teach us to feel, teach us to know,
Teach us in life and death to shew
    What treasures of grace are thine.

---

12. The Holy Guardian Angel.
(October 2nd.)

Kind Angel guardian, thanks to thee
For thy so watchful care of me;
Oh, lead me still in ways of truth,
Dear guide of childhood and of youth.

Kind Angel guardian, let my tears
Implore thee too for riper years;
Oh, keep me safe in wisdom's way,
And bring me back if I should stray.

When angry passions fill my soul,
Subdue them to thy meek control;
Through good and ill, oh, ever be
A guide, a guard, a friend to me.

And when death's hand shall seal mine eyes,
Oh, bear my spirit to the skies,
And teach me there my voice to raise
In hymns of never-ending praise.

22. Saint Teresa.

(October 15th.)

SWEET Saint, in thy young childhood's day
  The thought was in thy infant head,
That it were sweet to die for Christ,
  And for the faith thy blood to shed.

But God decreed thee not to fall
  By sword of Paynim, Turk, or Moor;
A living death of martyrdom
  His love reserv'd thee to endure.

Thy youthful follies oft deplor'd
  To us have made thee still more dear;
Since we in them have come to know
  Thy candour and thy truth sincere.

For when thy Lord, with sweet reproof,
  Had made to thee thine errors known,
At once thy frank and loving heart
  Was wholly kept for Him alone.

Oh, what a strange instructive scene
  Thy life thenceforth began to be!
Now suffering dread unheard-of pain,
  Now lost in wondrous ecstacy.

Now contemplating things divine,
  Beyond the power of man to tell;
Now in appalling vision plung'd,
  Amid the hopeless cries of hell.

O sweet Teresa, now at last,
  Thy labours o'er and heaven won,
Thou lovest God without restraint,
  And shinest brighter than the sun.

Ah, then, from thy fair throne above
  Obtain for us thy children here,
To imitate thy childhood's love,
  In after life to persevere.

---

23. Feast of the Immaculate Conception of the B. V. Mary.

(December 8th.)

Hail, Mary, only sinless child
  Of guilty Adam's fallen race ;
Conceiv'd all pure and undefil'd,
  Through thy dear Lord's preventing grace

He would not have the blight of sin
  A moment rest thy soul upon ;
For pure without, and pure within,
  Must be the Mother of His Son.

No haughty fiend might boast that he
  One moment held thee in his snare,
Who of the dread Divinity
  Wert destin'd for the Temple fair

So thou wert sinless in thy birth,
  And sinless after as before ;
The only creature of this earth
  Whom sin ne'er cast its shadow o'er.

O sweetest lily ! all untorn,
  Though nurs'd the thorns of earth among,
To thee we sigh, to thee we mourn,
  To thee we lift our suppliant song.

From Satan's snare preserve us free,
  And keep us safe from earthly stain,
That in this world we pure may be,
  And in the next may see thee reign.

O sweetest lily! all untorn,
    Though nurs'd the thorns of earth among
To thee we sigh, to thee we mourn,
    To thee we lift our suppliant song.

MISCELLANEOUS HYMNS.

---

24. An Ebening Hymn to the Blessed Virgin.

As the dewy shades of even
   Gather o'er the balmy air,
Listen, gentle Queen of Heav'n,
   Listen to my vesper prayer
Holy Mother, near me hover,
   Free my thoughts from aught defil'd;
With thy wings of mercy cover,
   Safe from harm, thy helpless child.

Thine own sinless heart was broken,
   Sorrow's sword had pierc'd it through;
Give, oh, give me some sweet token
   Of thy tender love so true.
Queen of sorrows, guard and guide me,
   Let me to thine arms repair;
In thy tender bosom hide me,
   Mary, take me to thy care,

25. A Child's Hymn to the Blessed Virgin.

MAIDEN Mother, meek and mild,
Take, oh, take me for thy child.
All my life, oh let it be
My best joy to think of thee.

When my eyes are clos'd in sleep
Through the night my slumbers keep,
Make my latest thought to be
How to love thy Son and thee.

Teach me when the sunbeam bright
Calls me with its golden light,
How my waking thoughts may be
Turn'd to Jesus and to thee.

And, oh, teach me through the day
Oft to raise my heart and say,
"Maiden Mother, meek and mild,
Guard, oh, guard thy little child!"

Thus, sweet Mother, day and night
Thou shalt guide my steps aright;
And my dying words shall be,
"Virgin Mother, pray for me!"

26. Star of Jacob.

STAR of Jacob, ever beaming
With a radiance all divine,
Mid the stars of highest heaven
Glows no purer ray than thine.

All in stoles of snowy whiteness,
   Unto thee the angels sing;
Unto thee the virgin choirs,—
   Mother of th' eternal King!

Joyful in thy path they scatter
   Roses white and lilies fair;
Yet with thy celestial beauty
   Rose nor lily may compare.

Oh, that this low earth of ours,
   Answ'ring to th' angelic strain,
With thy praises might re-echo,
   Till the heav'ns replied again.

27. Hail, thou Star of Ocean.

HAIL, thou Star of Ocean,
   Portal of the sky,
Ever Virgin Mother
   Of the Lord most high!

Oh, by Gabriel's Ave,
   Utter'd long ago,
Eva's name reversing,
   'Stablish peace below.

Break the captive's fetters,
   Light on darkness pour;
All our ills expelling,
   Every bliss implore.

Show thyself a mother,
   Offer Him our sighs;
Who for us incarnate
   Did not thee despise.

Virgin of all virgins,
 To thy shelter take us;
Gentlest of the gentle,
 Chaste and gentle make us.

Still as on we journey,
 Help our weak endeavour;
Till with thee and Jesus
 We rejoice for ever.

Through the highest heaven,
 To the all-holy Three,
Father, Son, and Spirit,
 One same glory be.

**28. Gratitude for the early
Knowledge of God.**

AMONG the gifts thy hands bestow
 Each day and hour on me,
'Tis not the least, O Lord, to know
 That they all come from Thee

How joyfully each day I ought
 Thy precepts to fulfil,
Since I have been so early taught
 To do thy gracious will!

I cannot tell thee what my heart
 Would have me say to thee,
For having taught me what Thou art,
 And what I ought to be.

O Saviour blest and God ador'd,
  Still keep me in Thy fear;
And in my teachers' words, O Lord,
  May I Thy voice revere.

---

29. Hymn to the Good Shepherd.

Loving Shepherd of Thy sheep,
Keep Thy lamb, in safety keep :
Nothing can Thy power withstand,
None can pluck me from Thy hand

Loving Shepherd, Thou didst give
Thine own life that I might live;
May I love Thee day by day,
Gladly Thy sweet will obey.

Loving Shepherd, ever near,
Teach Thy lamb Thy voice to hear;
Suffer not my steps to stray
From the straight and narrow way.

Where Thou leadest may I go,
Walking in Thy steps below;
Then before Thy Father's throne,
Jesu, claim me for Thine own.

---

30. Litany of the Birth of Jesus.

By the word to Mary giv'n,
By Thy first descent from heav'n,
By Thine infant form so fair,
Trembling in the midnight air,—

Chorus.

Babe of Bethlehem, hear our cry!
　Thou wert helpless once as we;
Hear the loving Litany
　We, Thy children, sing to Thee

By Thy poor and lowly lot,
By the manger and the grot,
By Thy little feet and hands,
Folded fast in swaddling bands,
　Babe of Bethlehem, &c.

By the worship shepherds paid,
By the gifts that sages made,
Gold and myrrh and incense sweet,
Laid in homage at Thy feet,—
　Babe of Bethlehem, &c.

By St. Joseph's thoughts amaz'd,
When he first upon Thee gaz'd,
And his Lord and Maker saw
Laid upon a bed of straw,—
  Babe of Bethlehem, &c.

And oh, more than all the rest,
By the joy of Mary's breast
When she, kneeling, first ador'd
Thee, her child and yet her Lord,—
  Babe of Bethlehem, &c.

---

31. Litany of the Childhood of Jesus.

By the name which Thou didst take,
Suffering early for our sake;
Name ador'd on bended knee,
Name of grace and majesty,—

Chorus.

Child of Mary, hear our cry!
  Thou wert little once as we;
Hear the loving Litany
  We, Thy children, sing to Thee

By the joy of Simeon blest,
When he clasp'd Thee to his breast:
By the widow'd Anna's song,
Pour'd amid the wondering throng,—
  Child of Mary, &c.

By Thine angel-bidden flight
Into Egypt in the night;

By Thy home at Herod s death
In despised Nazareth,—
    Child of Mary, &c.

By Thy tender mother's fears,
By her many sighs and tears,
As she sought Thee night and day,
Turning back upon her way,—
    Child of Mary, &c.

By her wond'ring love and awe,
In the temple when she saw
Thee, her child, so young and fair,
Wiser then the wisest there,—
    Child of Mary, &c.

32. Litany of the Passion of Jesus.

By the blood that flow'd from Thee
In Thy bitter agony,
By the scourge so meekly borne,
By Thy purple robe of scorn,—

Chorus.

Jesu, Saviour, hear our cry!
    Thou wert suffering once as we;
Hear the loving Litany
    We, Thy children, sing to Thee

By the thorns that crown'd Thy head,
By Thy sceptre of a reed,
By Thy footstep faint and slow,
Weigh'd beneath Thy cross of woe,—
    Jesu, Saviour, &c.

By the nails and pointed spear,
By Thy people's cruel jeer,
By Thy dying prayer which rose
Begging mercy for Thy foes,—
    Jesu, Saviour, &c.

By the darkness thick as night,
Blotting out the sun from sight;
By the cry with which in death
Thou didst yield Thy parting breath,—
    Jesu, Saviour, &c.

By Thy weeping mother's woe,
By the sword that pierc'd her through,
When in anguish standing by,
On the cross she saw Thee die,—
    Jesu, Saviour, &c.

33.   Litany of the Resurrection of Jesus.

By the first bright Easter-day,
When the stone was rolled away;

By the glory round Thee shed
At Thy rising from the dead,—

Chorus.

King of glory, hear our cry!
   Make us soon Thy joys to see;
Hear the loving Litany
   We, Thy children, sing to Thee

By Thy mother's fond embrace,
By her joy to see Thy face,
When, all bright in radiant bloom,
Thee she welcom'd from the tomb,—
　　King of glory, &c.

By the joy of Magdalen,
When she saw Thee once again,
And entranc'd in rapture sweet,
Knelt to kiss Thy sacred feet,—
　　King of glory, &c.

By their joy who greeted Thee
'Mid the hills of Galilee;
By Thy keys of might divine,
Vested in St. Peter's line,—
　　King of glory, &c

By Thy parting blessing giv'n
As Thou didst ascend to heav'n;
By the cloud of living light
That receiv'd Thee out of sight,—
　　King of glory, &c.

---

34. May Jesus Christ be praised.

WHEN morning gilds the skies,
My heart awaking cries,
　　May Jesus Christ be prais'd!
Alike at work and prayer,
To Jesus I repair:
　　May Jesus Christ be prais'd

The sacred minster bell,
It peals o'er hill and dell ·
  ·May, &c.
Oh, hark to what it sings,
As joyously it rings,
  May, &c.

When you begin the day,
Oh, never fail to say,
  May, &c.
And at your work rejoice
To sing with heart and voice,
  May, &c.

Be this at meals your grace,
In every time and place,
  May, &c.
Be this, when day is past,
Of all your thoughts the·last,
  May, &c.

To God the Word on high
The hosts of angels cry,
  May, &c.
Let children too upraise
Their voice in hymns of praise :
  May, &c.

Let earth's wide circle round
In joyful notes resound :
  May, &c.
Let air and sea and sky
Through depth and height reply,
  May Jesus Christ be prais'd!

35.   Divine Grace.

O JESU, my beloved King,
  I give all thanks to Thee,
Who by Thy cross hast merited
  Celestial grace for me.

In Adam rais'd to dignities
  Transcendent and divine;
In Adam fallen from the bliss
  That once in him was mine.—

That grace to which my native strength
  Could never have attain'd,
That grace, O my Incarnate God,
  In Thee I have regain'd.

O gift of love! O gift immense!
  Surpassing nature's law;
What force to will and to perform
  From this pure fount I draw.

By this how many passing acts,
  Which else had been in vain,
Endued with meritorious power
  A prize eternal gain!

By this to me is open'd wide,
  Through death's inviting door,
A brighter world, a nobler realm
  Than Adam lost of yore.

O Jesu! on whose grace alone
  I by Thy grace depend,
Grant me the grace to persevere
  In grace unto the end.

36. Mother of Mercy.

MOTHER of Mercy, day by day
  My love of thee grows more and more;
Thy gifts are strewn upon my way,
  Like sands upon the great sea-shore

Though poverty and work and woe
  The masters of my life may be;
In darkest hours, who does not know
  That all is light with love of thee?

Ah, little know they of thy worth
  Who would thy love deny to me;
For what did Jesus love on earth
  One-half so tenderly as thee?

Oh, gain me grace to love thee more;
  Thy Son will give if thou wilt plead:
And, Mother, when life's cares are o'er,
  Oh, I shall love thee then indeed.

My Lord, when His three hours were run,
  Bequeath'd thee from the cross to me;
And oh, how can I love thy Son,
  Sweet Mother, if I love not thee?

---

37. Faith of our Fathers.

FAITH of our fathers! living still,
  In spite of dungeon, fire, or sword;
Oh, how our hearts beat high with joy
  Whene'er we hear that glorious word!

Chorus.

Faith of our fathers! holy Faith!
We will be true to thee till death.

Our fathers chain'd in prisons dark,
  Were still in heart and conscience free,
How sweet would be their children's fate,
  If they like them could die for thee!
    Faith of our Fathers! &c.

Faith of our fathers! Mary's prayers
  Shall win our country back to thee,
And through the truth that comes from God,
  Oh, then indeed shall we be free.
    Faith of our Fathers! &c.

Faith of our Fathers! we will love
  Both friend and foe in all our strife,
And preach thee too, as love knows how,
  By kindly words and virtuous life.
    Faith of our Fathers! &c.

Faith of our Fathers! guile and force
  To do thee bitter wrong unite;
But England's saints shall fight for us,
  And bring us back thy blessed light.
    Faith of our Fathers! &c.

Faith of our Fathers.
(For Ireland.)

FAITH of our fathers! living still,
  In spite of dungeon, fire, and sword;
Oh, Ireland's hearts beat high with joy
  Whene'er they hear that glorious word.

· Faith of our fathers! holy Faith!
We will be true to thee till death!

Our fathers chain'd in prisons dark,
Were still in heart and conscience free;
How sweet would be their children's fate,
If they like them could die for thee!
Faith of our Fathers, &c.

Faith of our Fathers! Mary's prayers
Shall keep our country fast to thee;
And through the truth that comes from God,
Oh, we shall prosper and be free.
Faith of our Fathers! &c.

Faith of our Fathers! we will love
Both friend and foe in all our strife;
And preach thee too as love knows how,
By kindly words and virtuous life
Faith of our Fathers! &c.

Faith of our Fathers! guile and force
To do thee bitter wrong unite;
But Erin's saints shall fight for us,
And keep undimm'd thy blessed light.
Faith of our Fathers! &o.

---

38. 𝕿𝖍𝖊 𝖑𝖆𝖘𝖙 𝕱𝖆𝖗𝖊𝖜𝖊𝖑𝖑.

(A Hymn on Death.)

Come, my soul, and let us dwell
· On each ling'ring last farewell,

Which at no far distant day
Thou perforce wilt have to pay
To whatever here below
Shall have made thy joy or woe.

Fare ye well—I hear thee sigh—
Fare ye well, O earth and sky!
Morning's golden-tissued ray,
Changing hours of night and day,
Wood and valley, sea and shore,
I may see your face no more!

Fare ye well, affections vain,
Full of pleasure, full of pain;
Home and friends and kindred dear,
All that was my comfort here;
My poor eyes are closing fast,
Now I look on you my last.

Dimmer, dimmer grows the light!
Now 'tis thick descending night!
Oh, when next again I see,
What a sight awaiteth me!
Speechless standing all alone,
Right before the judgment throne

39. Hymn before the Image of Mary.

Holy Queen, we bend before thee,
Queen of purity divine;
Make us love thee, we implore thee,
Make us truly to be thine

Unto thee a Child was given,
   Greater than the sons of men;
Coming down from highest heaven,
   To create the world again.

Thou by faith the gates unfolding
   Of the kingdom in the skies,
Hast to us, by faith beholding,
   Shewn the land of Paradise.

Thou, when deepest night infernal
   Had for ages shrouded man,
Gavest us that light eternal
   Promis'd when the world began

Teach, oh teach us, holy Mother,
   How to conquer every sin,
How to love and help each other,
   How the prize of life to win.

Teach us how all earthly pleasures,
   All the world's enchanting bloom,
Are outrivall'd by the treasures
   Of the glorious world to come.

Oh, by that Almighty Maker,
   Whom thyself a virgin bore;
Oh, by thy supreme Creator,
   Link'd with thee for evermore,—

By the hope thy name inspires,
   By our doom revers'd through thee,
Bring us, Queen of angel choirs,
   To a blest eternity

40. Divine Providence.

BEHOLD the lilies of the field,
   They neither toil nor sow;
Yet God doth all things needful yield,
   That they may bud and blow.

Not Solomon in glory shone
   Like one of these poor flowers,
That look to God, and God alone,
   For sunshine and for showers.

And does His mercy value less
   The offspring of His grace?
And will a Father's love not bless
   The child that seeks His face?

Oh, then away with fear and care
   For all that may betide:
And turn to God in trustful pray'r,
   And in His love confide.

He is our Father and He knows
   His earthly children's need;
On all our daily wants and woes
   He looks with careful heed.

---

41. If e'er my heart in riper years.

IF e'er my heart in riper years
Shall beat with anguish, grief, or fears,
My Jesus He will hear each moan,
And gently say, "Thou'rt not alcre."

Though fled were every earthly friend
On whom I might or could depend

D

Though left by all, to all unknown,
He still will say, "Thou'rt not alone."

Though cherish'd ones around me die,
And sever'd be each earthly tie;
I still may seek my Saviour's throne,
And hear Him say, "Thou'rt not alone."

So too when all my years are past,
And life her race hath run at last,
My God, Thou wilt not me disown,
To whom Thou saidst, "Thou'rt not alone."

------

42. Hymn to Jesus in the Blessed Sacrament.

O Jesu, it were surely sweet
To sit and listen at Thy feet,
With those who in Thy life drew near
Thy words of wondrous grace to hear.

And it were sweet to walk with Thee
Along the shores of Galilee;
Or, safe embark'd in Peter's boat,
O er its blue waves with Thee to float.

Yet sweeter far it is to pray
Before Thine altar night and day,
And feel the love which bids Thee lie
Thus wrapt in holiest mystery.

Yes; Jesus! Thou art hidden thus
On this poor earth for love of us;
And yet upon Thine altar-throne,
Too oft we leave Thee all alone.

Ah, since it is Thy chief delight
To dwell with us both day and night,
Sweet Jesus make it ours to be
Both night and day to stay with Thee.

43. Hymn of Thanksgiving after Communion.

WHAT happiness can equal mine?
I've found the object of my love;
My Saviour and my Lord divine
Is come to me from heav'n above.
He makes my heart His own abode.
His flesh becomes my daily bread
He pours on me His healing blood,
And with His life my soul is fed.

My love is mine, and I am His;
In me He dwells, in Him I live:
Where could I taste a purer bliss?
What greater boon could Jesus give!
O royal banquet! heav'nly feast!
O flowing fount of life and grace!
Where God the Giver, man the guest,
Meet and unite in sweet embrace.

Dear Jesus, now my heart is Thine,
Oh, may it never from Thee fly;
My God, be Thou for ever mine,
And I Thine own eternally.
No more, O Satan, thee I fear!
O world, thy charms I now despise.
For Christ himself is with me here,
My joy, my life, my paradise.

44. Hymn of Thanksgiving after Communion.

(II.)

Ah! what is this enchanting calm
  Which thus with peace my bosom fills,
Which o er my spirit pours a balm,
  And through my inmost being thrills?

Is there some seraph hither sent,
  Diffusing sweetness from his wings,
To steep my bosom in content
  Unknown, unfelt, from earthly things?

No! something purer far must dwell
  Within this raptured soul of mine;
'Tis what no mortal tongue can tell,
  Tis more than heavenly, 'tis divine

My God! my Jesus! it is Thou
  Art ravishing my heart with bliss;
Thy presence is within me now:
  Ah! could I ask a boon like this?

Yes! stooping from Thy throne above,
  Thou wilt not dwell from man apart;
Thy dearest home becomes, through love,
  The tabernacle of my heart.

45. Hymn to the Blessed Sacrament.

Jesus! my Lord, my God, my all!
  How can I love Thee as I ought?
And how revere this wondrous gift
  So far surpassing hope or thought?

Sweet Sacrament! we thee adore!
Oh, make us love thee more and more!

Had I but Mary's sinless heart
To love Thee with, my dearest King,
Oh, with what bursts of fervent praise
Thy goodness, Jesus, would I sing
Sweet Sacrament, &c.

Oh, see! within a creature's hand
The vast Creator deigns to be,
Reposing infant-like, as though
On Joseph's arm, or Mary's knee.
Sweet Sacrament, &c.

Thy Body, Soul, and Godhead, all!
Oh, mystery of love divine!
I cannot compass all I have;
For all Thou hast and art are mine!
Sweet Sacrament, &c.

He comes! He comes! the Lord of Hosts,
Borne on His throne triumphantly!
We see Thee, and we know Thee, Lord;
And yearn to shed our blood for Thee
Sweet Sacrament, &c.

---

46. Hail to Thee, true Body.

HAIL to Thee, true Body, sprung
'From the Virgin Mary's womb;
The same that on the Cross was hung,
And bore for man the bitter doom.

Thou whose side was pierc'd and flow'd,
Both with water and with blood;
Suffer us to taste of Thee,
In our life's last agony.
O kind, O loving One,
O sweet Jesu, Mary's Son!

47. Hymn to the Sacred Heart.

To Christ, the Prince of Peace,
And Son of God most high,
The Father of the world to come,
Sing we with holy joy.

Deep in His Heart for us
The wound of love He bore;—
That love, which still He kindles in
The hearts that Him adore.

O Jesu! Victim blest!
What else but love divine
Could Thee constrain to open thus
That sacred Heart of Thine?

O Fount of endless life!
O Spring of waters clear!
O Flame celestial, cleansing all
Who unto Thee draw near!

Hide me in Thy dear Heart,
For thither do I fly;
There seek Thy grace through life, in death
Thine immortality.

Praise to the Father be,
Praise to His only Son;
Praise to the blessed Paraclete,
While endless ages run.

48. Hymn to the Sacred Wounds of Jesus.

God of mercy let us run
  Where yon fount of sorrow flows,
Pondering sweetly one by one,
  Jesu's wounds and Mary's woes.

Ah! those tears our Lady shed,
  Enough to drown a world of sin;
Tears that Jesu's sorrows fed,
  Peace and pardon well may win.

His five wounds a very home
  For our prayers and praises prove;
And our Lady's woes become
  Endless joys in Heaven above.

Jesu, who for us didst die,
  All on Thee our love we pour;
And in the Holy Trinity
  Worship Thee for evermore.

49. Hymn to the Precious Blood.

Hail, Jesus! hail! who for my sake
Sweet Blood from Mary's veins didst take,
  And shed it all for me;
Oh, blessed be my Saviour's Blood,
My life, my light, my only good,
  To all eternity.

To endless ages let us praise
The Precious Blood whose price could raise
  The world from wrath and sin;

Whose streams our inward thirst appease,
And heal the sinner's worst disease,
  If he but bathe therein.

Oh, to be sprinkled from the wells
Of Christ's own sacred Blood excels
  Earth's best and highest bliss:
The ministers of wrath divine
Hurt not the happy hearts that shine
  With those red drops of His.

Ah, there is joy amid the Saints,
And hell's despairing courage faints,
  When this sweet song we raise:
Oh, louder then, and louder still,
Earth with one mighty chorus fill,
  The Precious Blood to praise!

---

50. Sing, Sing, ye Angel Bands.

SING, sing, ye Angel bands,
  All beautiful and bright;
For higher still, and higher,
  Through the vast fields of light,
Mary, your Queen ascends,
  Like the sweet moon at night.

A fairer flower than she
  On earth hath never been;
And, save the throne of God,
  Your heav'ns have never seen
A wonder half so bright
  As your ascending Queen.

O happy Angels! look,
  How beautiful she is!

See! Jesus bears her up,
　Her hand is lock'd in His;
Oh, who can tell the height
　Of that fair Mother's bliss

And shall I lose thee, then,
　Lose my sweet right to thee
Ah, no!—the Angel's Queen
　Man's mother still will be;
And thou, upon thy throne,
　Will keep thy love for me

---

51. Mother of Almighty God.

Mother of Almighty God,
　Suppliant at thy feet we pray;
Shelter us from Satan's fraud,
　Safe beneath thy wing this day.

'Twas by reason of our fall,
　In our first forefather's crime,
That the mighty Lord of all
　Rais'd thee to thy rank sublime.

Oh, then upon Adam's race
　Look thou with a pitying eye;
And entreat of Jesu's grace,
　Till he lay his anger by.

Honour, virtue, glory, merit,
　Be to Thee, O Virgin's Son,
With the Father and the Spirit,
　While eternal ages run.

---

52. The Help of Christians.

Mother of our Lord and Saviour,
First in beauty as in power,

Glory of the Christian nations,
  Ready help in trouble's hour.

Though the gates of Hell against us,
  With profoundest fury rage;
Though the ancient foe assault us,
  And his fiercest battle wage.

Nought can hurt the pure in spirit,
  Who upon thine aid rely;
At thy hand secure of gaining
  Strength and mercy from on high

Through the everlasting ages,
  Blessed Trinity, to Thee,
Father, Son, and Holy Spirit,
  Praise and endless glory be

---

58. Stabat Mater.

At the Cross her station keeping,
Stood the mournful mother weeping,
  Close to Jesus to the last.
Through her heart, His sorrow sharing,
All His bitter anguish bearing,
  Now at length the sword had pass'd.

Oh, how sad and sore distress'd
Was that Mother, highly blest
  Of the sole begotten One!
Christ above in torment hangs;
She beneath beholds the pangs
  Of her dying glorious Son.

Is there one who would not weep,
Whelmed in miseries so deep,
  Christ's dear Mother to behold?
Can the human heart refrain

From partaking in her pain,
  In that Mother's pain untold?

Bruised, derided, cursed, defiled,
She beheld her tender Child
  All with bloody scourges rent;
For the sins of His own nation,
Saw Him hang in desolation,
  Till His Spirit forth He sent.

O thou Mother! fount of love!
Touch my spirit from above,
  Make my heart with thine accord:
Make me feel as thou hast felt;
Make my soul to glow and melt
  With the love of Christ my Lord.

Holy Mother! pierce me through;
In my heart each wound renew
  Of my Saviour crucified;
Let me share with thee His pain,
Who for all my sins was slain,
  Who for me in torments died.

Let me mingle tears with thee,
Mourning Him who mourn'd for me,
  All the days that I may live:
By the Cross with thee to stay;
There with thee to weep and pray;
  Is all I ask of thee to give.

Virgin of all virgins best!
Listen to my fond request:
  Let me share thy grief divine;
Let me, to my latest breath,
In my body bear the death
  Of that dying Son of thine.

54. Hymn to the Seben Dolours of the Blessed Virgin.

WHAT a sea of bitter sorrows
  Did the soul of Mary toss;
To and fro upon its billows,
  While she wept her bitter loss,
In her arms her Jesus holding,
  Torn but newly from the Cross!

O that mournful Virgin Mother!
  See her tears how fast they flow
Down upon His mangled body
  Wounded side, and thorny brow;
While His hands and feet she kisses—
  Picture of immortal woe!

Oft and oft His arms and bosom
  Fondly straining to her own;
Oft her pallid lips imprinting
  On each wound of her dear Son;
Till at last in swoons of anguish,
  Sense and consciousness are gone.

Gentle Mother, we beseech thee,
  By thy tears and troubles sore;
By the death of thy dear Offspring;
  By the bloody wounds He bore;
Touch our hearts with that true sorrow
  Which afflicted thee of yore

To the Father everlasting,
  And the Son, who reigns on high,
With the coëternal Spirit,
  Trinity in Unity,
Be salvation, honour, blessing,
  Now and through eternity.

55. Hymn of St. Francis Xavier.

My God, I love Thee, not because
  I hope for Heaven thereby;
Nor because they who love Thee not,
  Must burn eternally.

Thou, O my Jesus, Thou didst me
  Upon the Cross embrace;
For me didst bear the nails and spear,
  And manifold disgrace;

And griefs and torments numberless,
  And sweat of agony;
E'en death itself—and all for one
  Who was Thine enemy.

Then why, O blessed Jesus Christ!
  Should I not love Thee well?
Not for the sake of winning Heaven,
  Or of escaping Hell;

Not with the hope of gaining aught;
  Not seeking a reward;
But, as Thyself hast loved me,
  O ever-loving Lord.

E'en so I love Thee, and will love,
  And in Thy Praise will sing;
Solely because Thou art my God,
  And my eternal King.

56. Hymn for the Month of May.

GREEN are the leaves, and sweet the flowers,
  And rich the hues of May;
We see them in the gardens round,
  And market-paniers gay:

And e'en among our streets and lanes,
  And alleys, we descry,
By fitful gleams, the fair sunshine,
  The blue transparent sky.

Chorus.

O Mother-maid, be thou our aid,
  Now in the opening year;
Lest sights of earth to sin give birth,
  And bring the tempter near.

Green is the grass, but wait awhile;
  'Twill grow, and then-will wither;
The flowrets, brightly as they smile,
  Shall perish altogether:
The merry sun, you sure would say,
  It ne'er could set in gloom;
But earth's best joys have all an end,
  And sin a heavy doom.

Chorus.

But Mother-maid, thou dost not fade;
  With stars above thy brow,
And the pale moon beneath thy feet
  For ever throned art thou.

The green green grass, the glittering grove,
  The heaven's majestic dome,
They image forth a tenderer bower,
  A more refulgent home;
They tell us of that paradise
  Of everlasting rest,
And that high Tree, all flowers and fruit,
  The sweetest yet the best.

Chorus.

O Mary pure and beautiful,
Thou art the Queen of May;
Our garlands wear about thy hair,
And they will ne'er decay.

---

57. Hail, Queen of Heaven.

HAIL, Queen of Heav'n, the ocean Star,
Guide of the wand'rer here below!
Thrown on life's surge we claim thy care,
Save us from peril and from woe.
Mother of Christ, Star of the sea,
Pray for the wanderer, pray for me

O gentle, chaste, and spotless Maid,
We sinners make our prayers through thee
Remind thy Son that He has paid
The price of our iniquity.
Virgin most pure, Star of the sea,
Pray for the sinner, pray for me.

Sojourners in this vale of tears,
To thee, blest Advocate, we cry,
Pity our sorrows, calm our fears,
And soothe with hope our misery.
Refuge in grief, Star of the sea,
Pray for the mourner, pray for me.

58.   Veni Creator.

Come, O Creator Spirit blest!
And in our souls take up Thy rest;
Come, with Thy grace and heav'nly aid,
To fill the hearts which Thou hast made

Great Paraclete! to Thee we cry:
O highest gift of God most high!
O fount of life! O fire of love!
And sweet Anointing from above!

Thou in thy sevenfold gifts art known;
Thee Finger of God's hand we own;
The promise of the Father Thou!
Who dost the tongue with pow'r endow.

Kindle our senses from above,
And make our hearts o'erflow with love;
With patience firm, and virtue high,
The weakness of our flesh supply

Far from us drive the foe we dread,
And grant us Thy true peace instead,
So shall we not, with Thee for guide,
Turn from the path of life aside.

Oh, may Thy grace on us bestow,
The Father and the Son to know;
And Thee through endless times confess'd
Of both, th' eternal Spirit blest.

All glory while the ages run
Be to the Father and the Son
Who rose from death; the same to Thee,
O Holy Ghost eternally.